Adrenaline for the New Year

Adrenaline for the New Year

Table Of Contents

Foreword

In this e-book, you'll be getting the best personal growth information to supercharge your New Year that I've collected over the past numerous years, combined with my own experiences and mental attitude towards life, prepared over a period of several months, until now, when you're holding my most scrumptious personal growth formula in your hands!

I've nailed down everything I know about getting the most out of life to the most crucial steps. The things that will really alter your life!

Every single chapter you're about to study is thickly packed with info. I don't believe in fluffing about and duplicating my point 12 times. I likewise don't wish you to get bored. Hey, becoming bored isn't fun, and having fun while developing is what this e-book is all about!

New Year Adrenaline

How to take advantage of the New Year and blast forward into the future with new energy and accomplishments.

Chapter 1:

Begin With The Body

Synopsis

O.K.! Let's get moving! Before we progress to the super-exciting things about your brain, let's take on the mildly energizing stuff about your body. Since having your body well addressed provides you a lot of energy and less misdirection. It's similar to cooking - even the finest recipe won't do you much good if your pan has holes in it.

So let's first attend to any likely "holes" in your body by which your energy or centering get drained, and we'll be prepared to do the true magic!

Physical

Have you ever heard the older saying, "There's a fit brain in a fit body?" Yes, I understand, expressions are bothersome - after all they're primarily utilized by parents to make you accomplish things you don't wish to do. Like eat the right foods (ugh), go to bed early (ugh.), or go to school (ugh!). However by pure happenstance, this saying happens to be truthful!

Your mind only takes up five percent of your body mass... Even so it uses up twenty percent of the oxygen! You require a pretty efficient way of getting oxygen and glucose to the mind if you wish to utilize your mind to its full potential. Thankfully, you have got the blood flow.

The blood shifts the stuff to your brain. So you require a great and efficient blood flow to keep your brain alert and full of power. Slothful slow blood flow will not do you good.

And that's where physical exertion comes in. When you work out regularly (particularly aerobic exercise, like running or swimming), your blood flow betters. You get more blood flowing, and it transmits nutrients more efficiently. You'll be able to concentrate longer, and think clearer.

Hold on! Don't place your hands up in repulsion just because I mention "physical exertion"! I'll show you that it may be fun as well as truly healthy!

After a couple of days without exercise, I commonly begin to get edgy and somewhat cranky. And thank you to science, I understand why, and what to do about it. Daily, you encounter a few nerve-racking situations that discharge adrenaline into your blood stream. Your body does not realize the difference between a tiger and a huge work assignment. Both set off adrenaline release. You'll have to burn off this unneeded adrenaline someway.

You may either wait for it to build up, then blow a fuse and throw your PC monitor out the window (make certain you've a video camera convenient if you pick this route). Or you may simply exercise every 2 or 3 days.

Exercise burns off the extra adrenaline that you discharge during a normal day. It likewise releases endorphins, the body's innate opiates. This provides you the warm, pleased feeling you get after a great sweaty work out session.

I'm not a huge fan of going to the gymnasium. So I make my work out fun! I call some acquaintances for a game of hoops, or do some park training, or run to the yoga club, or anything else I like.

When you acquire your exercise in an amusing way, not only do you get all the health Advantages, but you likewise truly enjoy it! Naturally, if you like hitting the gym, then do it!

Commonly, authorities seem to think aerobics is the truly crucial thing for your health. Put differently, working out your heart and lungs, in addition to your exterior muscles.

You are able to recognize aerobics really easily. If you continue, you run out of breath. With muscle building, your muscles become tired before you run out of breath.

Or, you are able to take on this approach one of my acquaintances utilizes. He calls it mammalian work out:

Do what you enjoy, when you wish, precisely as you like it, simply for fun. Just like youngsters and mammals. No ridiculous exercise program to tell you what you'll be doing 2 weeks from now.

Doesn't that simply sound amazing?

If you don't take a breath properly, you won't be happy. Truly. As a matter of fact, studies show that a hundred percent of all content individuals breathe properly.

Breathing correctly is supremely crucial. The yogis have analyzed the art of breathing for centuries, and have dedicated a whole discipline to breathing the right way. I've done a few yogi breathing exercises, and I can tell you its potent stuff. But you don't have to believe in any eastern religious thingy to breathe correctly. There's a great deal of Western scientific evidence for great breathing.

Incidentally, did you ever observe that every major faith involves singing? Singing gets you taking a breath deeply and slowly, which are precisely the 2 correct characteristics that let proper gas exchange happen. Religions wish you to be content when you're in your church service/mosque/whatever, so you'll continue going there. It likewise explains the older folk wisdom - when you're feeling blue, sing a song. Surely, songs do more than make you take a breath properly, but that's a huge part of it.

So how do you get taking a breath properly?

When we take a breath shallowly, old air gets built up in the lungs. And each fresh breath only thins out that old air in your lungs. You won't get really fresh air in till you void your lungs of the stale old air.

In the west, we believe that each breath begins with inhaling. However Yogis claim that each breath begins with exhaling. As if you've a glass of muddied water, and wish to fill it with clean water instead... you first must empty the glass.

So begin right now by exhaling really slowly and totally. At the end, contract your tummy muscles to truly thrust out every last morsel of air.

Then simply hold your breath for a couple of moments with empty lungs. Once you begin feeling a physical impulse to inhale again, go for it! Ideally, you'll be beginning each breath with your   stomach. This   demonstrates that you're   taking a breath with your diaphragm, which is a sort of muscular wall between your chest and your tummy.

If you take a breath only by enlarging your chest, you're vastly under using your lung capability. Taking a breath with your diaphragm isn't only the simplest way to get air into your lungs; it likewise helps to get older blood from all over your body back into the heart. Your heart thrusts out the fresh blood. Your diaphragm brings in the utilized blood. So breathing suitable deep breaths is the most beneficial way to prevent a whole bunch of vein issues.

Food is madly crucial for your energy state. The great news is, I won't be pushing you into some loony diet. As a matter of fact, I'll let you pick out your diet! I'm certain you've went through the sluggishness and laziness you feel after a big meal. This is when all the blood pulls from your brain and into your tummy. A big lunch will leave you not able to think profoundly for about two - three hours. But hold on great news! You are able to avoid that sluggishness by consuming littler meals!

I never accepted the artificial 3-meals-a-day design. I normally eat when I'm hungry, and quit eating when I'm not hungry any longer. On my ideal days, when I've great access to great food, I eat approximately five - six times a day. This quashes big digestion drainage, and it likewise provides me with ceaseless supply of energy.

Now I'm not stating that it may be ideal for you (though dietary authorities support the 5-meals-a-day regimen). But if you feel like you need to eat at 3 set times a day simply because society is forcing you... don't. Eat when you wish and what you wish. This takes me to the following point.

What to consume? In a captivating experiment executed in the 30s, men of science gave a group of toddlers limitless 24/7 access to a huge range of foods from ice cream to spinach, basically letting them produce their own diet over a period of 30 days based on nothing more than their own feel of what they wished to eat and when.

The consequence? In spite of fluctuations in timing, chronological sequence and frequency, each youngster in the study wound up picking out what was considered to be a "balanced" diet over the month.

Our bodies are a lot brighter than we provide them credit for. If we'd simply heed them more often. Thankfully, I've got an easy trick for you to accomplish just that!

Picking out your diet.

Here's a easy 2 - step method to determine which foods are correct for you personally:
1. Consume a food.

2. Observe how you feel 1 hour afterwards. If you feel clear and industrious, you've consumed a food that's correct for you. If you don't, you have not.

Chapter 2:

Being Aware

Synopsis

O.K.! With your body addressed, the opening move for your brain is... Getting aware!

In this chapter, you'll discover (among additional things): the number 1 skill needed for psychological maturation (without this skill, you won't mature)how to exercise the brain like a muscle, becoming better at it each day how to pull out valuable lessons from your experiences even days after they occurred, and commit them to your subconscious. An easy yet mighty strategy to build your awareness each time you walk down the street.

The Brain

So what is awareness? I address it as "awareness", a few individuals address it as "living consciously", analysts call it "observing ego". Don't fret about the buzz words. It's still the same matter.

It essentially means being cognizant of what's happening around you and in your life, and measuredly selecting all your actions. Without awareness, you'll be enduring your whole life on automatic pilot. Like this person:

He experienced a period where he was dispirited quite a bit. He'd awake in the morning and his entire day would be pretty much destroyed by depression. Then, one day, he arose, and his brain began doing its thing. He decided he was simply gonna let it do its thing awhile and watch. So he positioned in bed, and simply sort of paid attention and produced some notes.

He sat there for approximately an hour. And he recognized, as he observed it intermittently that it was thinking of things he didn't wish to have occur, things that he didn't like and centering on that he wished to be where he wasn't. And that would pretty much smash his entire day.

Awe, I understand. Poor person.

Or, as I don't know where he lives, let's simply utilize him to exemplify a point. There's a person who at the start wasn't aware in the least. He was essentially running his whole life on automatic pilot, simply allowing the depression to get the better of him. Then one day, he recognized what was happening, and was like "plenty is plenty".

It's like he simply woke up. Like when the hypnotizer snaps his fingers and you abruptly became aware of real life. Now, he had a waking up. But it's astonishing how frequently little awakenings happen to all of us.

Do you wish to change something? You 1st have to become aware of it! Put differently, cognizance is the number 1 achievement that allows psychological development.

For instance, let's suppose you had to travel back and forth to work each morning. Further, let's suppose you'd forever take the same road, get lodged in rush-hour traffic, become furious at the traffic, then get apprehensive as you'd be late for work. Then, the following day, you'd leave your home at the same time and take the same road, get lodged in traffic once more, and the whole procedure would repeat itself.

That's a life without awareness. With awareness, after two or three times, you'd recognize that you're forever getting lodged in traffic, and do something about it. You'd attempt taking another route, or leave sooner, pull off flexible working hours to head off the rush hour traffic, or simply acquire some audio books and podcasts to hear in the car and utilize your time efficiently.

As you elevate your awareness of what's occurring around you (and inside you), you'll begin to amass useful lessons and learn as you go through living. You'll be accumulating valuable feedback from each situation.

And, candidly, awareness is amusing. When you're in a social locale, and may tell who likes who, who's pulled to who, etc. Or when you happen to be speaking to some furious individual, and you're thinking "I understand exactly why you're furious. If you'd simply quit shouting and take a good long view at your life, you'd recognize you detest your line of work!" Or if individuals disapprove of your actions, and you are able to think "I understand precisely why I'm doing this, and I understand it's the correct thing to do."Regrettable if you don't like it."

Awareness is truly composed of 2 bits. Common cognizance of your life, where you're going, and what you'd wish to better. Then awareness in the present moment.

They're 2 dissimilar sides of the same coin, and have to be tackled a bit differently. To gain common cognizance of your life, it helps to consider your life, contemplate, and perhaps write things down.

To get aware in the present moment, it helps to escape your head, stop examining so much, and rather just live in the present moment. Observe your surroundings. Observe what you are able to feel and see and hear with all your 5 senses. Observe what's occurring around you. Notice details that other people may overlook. Simply escape your head. Be in the present moment. As long as you've your awareness up and executing, you are able to forever think back over your experiences once you're back home, and pull all the lessons.

Journaling is good for getting aware of your life as a whole.

It essentially means authoring a diary. This lets you recap your progress, feel great about the great matters in your life, and work out

how you are able to better other bits of your life. I didn't trust it
initially, but putting things down is a crazily powerful strategy.
Somehow, once you put down stuff, something shifts in your brain.
You never have to study the writing again. The simple act of putting it
down lets it dip deep into your subconscious mind, and gets it
arranged. I frequently put down my goals for that precise reason.

It's difficult to say how frequently you ought to journal or how much
to put down. I commonly pick up a journal when there's something
truly huge occurring in my life, and I wish to capture all the life
lessons I may. I favor utilizing pen and paper, and evidently so do
most other individuals. But if journaling on a PC works for you, that's
ok. Put down as much as you feel you require. You are able to write
long complicated prose, or little bullet points.

Acknowledging the moment. Look upwards!
For a long time, I used to walk about looking at my feet. And then,
one day, I read it's a truly cool thought to really look upwards and
around when walking. So the following time I walked, I looked up.

I was like "scream"! The world looks so amazing when you quit
looking at your feet!" I'd simply look in the distance, and a mere walk
down the road would turn into a heroic movie scene. I likewise utilize
this as a metaphor for living as a whole. Life is amazing when you
begin noticing it. When you "take your eyes off the ground" life get to
be so much richer!

As I kept my gaze off the ground, and walked about like that more and
more, I began observing things. Acquaintances would nod and greet
me from the distance. Plenty of individuals would make eye contact
and grin as we became closer. I realized there's lots of eye contact

wanting to happen to you. You simply have to keep your eyes off the ground.

And it's the same in living. There's lots of "eye contact" that wishes to happen to you. Individuals wish to know you. Organizations wish to work with you. Successful individuals would like to give advice to you. But you'll overlook all that if you keep looking at your feet. So peek up, and make the opening move of approaching somebody. Life is too short to be spent viewing your feet.

Chapter 3:

Be Curious

Synopsis

Wonder is like the sparkplug that starts up your car's engine. Without that little spark of curiosity, the entire engine of your brain will simply be sitting idle and watching sitcom reruns. However if you let that spark carry you away, you'll grow and better quicker than you ever dreamt.

Fresh Eyes

If I discover a cool new thing, I question how it works, and how come it works. I'm not simply hungry for knowledge. I'm also curious about skills - I'm forever attempting fresh skills I never liked before, to see if anything captures my interest. Among the most beneficial things I've ever done for myself were speechmaking classes.

The great news is, you've all the curiosity you require inside you. If you discover yourself simply carrying out living, not truly caring about sampling new stuff, it simply means you aren't utilizing it. Curiosity is like a muscle - if you're not utilizing it often, it will get weaker, and you may even forget it's there. But it's still there, and merely utilizing it makes it more potent. Which means becoming curious about anything will better your life!

Among the most amazing things you are able to do for yourself is pump up your wonder... and it doesn't matter what you're curious about.

So how can you pump up your wonder?
Give it a little thought. Certainly there's something in your life you're curious about, however you don't let yourself give it an attempt. Perhaps you're stating things like "Oh, I'm a matured man today, I can't go around constructing a kite and playing with it in."

Or perhaps you can't think about anything recent that got your curiosity. Simply give it a little thought; there will be something from your past. There forever is. Perhaps you wished to study Spanish but you never did it? Perhaps you forever marveled about rock-climbing?

Becoming curious about things is good... but wonder without action is simply daydreaming. Don't get me wrong, daydreaming is amazing. But true lasting shifts come from following up on your curiosity!

Exuberance rocks! You understand, that feeling that you are able to take on the world. Once you jump headlong into a hard software project or a hobby, and defeat incredibly huge obstacles.

I've heard many self-improvement authorities talk about amping up your exuberance. Yeah, it's possible. But artificially produced enthusiasm commonly blows out in a couple of days. It's like placing paper in your hearth. Good to get the fire started, However before you realize it, the glare is gone, and you're left with simply a pile of ashes.

There are 3 solutions to that issue:
1. Exuberance backed by wonder
If you're unrelentingly curious about a matter, your enthusiasm will remain right there. Rather than an unnaturally produced exuberance, this is true and sustainable. As long as your wonder is there, the exuberance will stay.
2. An ablaze desire
If you've an ablaze desire to accomplish something, a desire so potent you'd be willing to walk across the desert to accomplish it, then you'll make true sustainable betterments to your life.
3. Habits
When you get a fire started up with paper, you commonly switch to burning wood. It lasts long and supplies lots of strong warmth. And that's what habits accomplish. They produce the true lasting shifts in your life.

Chapter 4:

Making Habits

Synopsis

Recall what I told you last chapter? That exuberance alone won't land big positive changes to your life? I used to become truly enthusiastic whenever I heard a fresh personal growth idea. After 2 weeks, once the initial fervor wore off, I quit. Wonder is amazing. Exhilaration is grand. But your life will be nothing but little bursts of exhilaration, unless you can leverage them to produce long-run positive shifts in your life.

Make It Usual

This is where habits come in!

Ceasing a minor habit like sleeping late is an order of magnitude simpler than quitting an addiction like smoking. If you've many habits you wish to alter, I suggest beginning with one that's easy, but meaningful. Establish confidence utilizing the 30-day trial run before attempting to tackle the hardest steps.

What is an easy change? An easy change may be huge or small, but it has a couple of ingredients that make it especially well-suited for this:

1. it's something you do daily.
2. it's something you accomplish in the same way, daily. (E.g. Rising in the morning)
3. it's an aboveboard improvement. This is more subjective, but it implies that there aren't going to be great, painful side-effects to shifting a behavior.
4. it's something you intend to be lasting. It's harder to be motivated to make a lasting shift than one you only expect to last a month.
5. You understand clearly whether you're sticking to your change or not. Physical exertion is a yes-no question. Either you go to the gymnasium or you don't. Being friendly is far more subjective and more difficult to do.

Your first change ought to fulfill most, if not all, of those criteria. But, most especially, it ought to be something you regard meaningful. If you don't see the shift as crucial, you won't seat the energy for a whole month.

Willpower isn't commonly the greatest issue with going an entire month. Occasionally you'll have to utilize your self-control to drudge your way through. But, more frequently, the greater issue is merely blanking out the trial run.

Blanking out a trial run and accidentally missing a day or two is more usual when the trial run is simple. Take something easy, like reading for quarter-hour a day. This may seem like a simple trial run. But somehow, it's a harder trial run to complete than reading for an hour a day. How come? Because a quarter-hour is forgettable.

Pick shifts that are hard to forget.

Only one habit at a time. Do less in your trial run than you think possible. Deliberately do less than you feel you're capable of. By restricting yourself, you'll avoid the typical issue of burning out in the first week or two.

Putting down the habit is like constituting a contract between you and your next self. If you don't write it down, the future you are more likely to desert the contract when matters get hard. Having a written account likewise lets you keep track of what you've accomplished in the past, so you are able to monitor them.

Fixation is your friend with this. If you are able to get obsessed about a shift for at least one month, you've much better odds to last the whole month. Missing focus or interest after the beginning few weeks is a basic issue.

30 days is an approximate estimate, not a scientifically exact number. 30 days is about what it takes to build a habit that no more requires

ceaseless vigilance. But that depends upon many factors. If your habit is infrequent, discrepant or too varied, it may take more than a calendar month.

- 28 -

After you complete your trial run, review your habit and ask yourself whether you've been doing it almost mechanically for the last week. If the answer is nope, and the shift is crucial, you may want to follow up one trial run with a different identical one, consecutively.

Mechanically here doesn't mean you're executing it in your sleep. By, mechanically I imply that it feels like an innate part of your routine. You're at the point where you're tolerable about continuing or quitting.

Chapter 5:

Carry Through

Synopsis

You've got through to the holy peak! The matchless matter that will let you metamorphose all your dreams into reality.

Carry through.

Action

It doesn't matter if you've read 100s of books of theory, and went to dozes of classes. Without carry through, you haven't truly done anything as yet.

There are 2 sorts of individuals regarding action. Those who like to have things worked out and be well fixed before taking action, almost to the point of being excessively analytical. Then there are those who merely jump into things headlong, and correct their path along the way.

The bad news is, individuals in the 2nd group are commonly more successful. As if you had to pick between studying about riding a bike, or simply jumping on one and learning by trial run and error, the 2nd way will be far faster and better.

And now for the goodness news! Theory solely isn't really valuable. Practice solely is pretty great. But once you blend theory AND practice, you're gonna succeed. And since somebody who does practice solely will do fairly well, they won't feel such a need to go acquire the theory. So you'll wind up with the best of both worlds.

Now you simply need to formulate the habit of taking action. As we already took on habits, that part won't be too difficult. And combining theory with practice, you are able to accomplish anything!

If you wait to be 100% certain prior to taking action, you'll be waiting eternally.

We learn best by acting. A few bright folks did a study on marketers, to work out what the top ones are doing differently from the rest. What separates the top 5% from the 95% is the speed of execution.

Certainly, there are times when you can't jump in headlong and correct your course along the way. But those events are pretty obvious, and in the huge majority of other cases, fast action is the way to go! Don't be afraid to take action. Make your conclusion fast; take action, and then make the essential fine-tunes along the way.

Simply make a decision. Because each time you make a conclusion, you learn something. You acquire feedback from the world. Arriving at a decision... Whatever decision... is greater than making no decision at all!

Wrapping Up

For the following 30 days, take one action each AND every day toward your most crucial goal.

And as you take action toward your goals daily, you develop the habit of taking action. You develop momentum. Taking action toward your goals becomes easier each day. Before you know it, you'll have completely altered your life.

And with that thought, I'll leave you. It's time to stop reading, and start DOING!

Get out there and take some action!